John

A Jesuit in Disguise (1579-1615)

To Commemorate
the 400th Anniversary of
St John Ogilvie's Martyrdom
at Glasgow Cross, Scotland

by
Eleanor McDowell

*All booklets are published thanks to the
generous support of the members of the
Catholic Truth Society*

CATHOLIC TRUTH SOCIETY

PUBLISHERS TO THE HOLY SEE

Contents

All rights reserved. First published 2015 by The Incorporated Catholic Truth Society, 40-46 Harleyford Road London SE11 5AY Tel: 020 7640 0042 Fax: 020 7640 0046. © The Incorporated Catholic Truth Society.

ISBN 978 1 78469 027 4

Preface

If "a life told is a life remembered" it is in this dignified spirit that this account of St John Ogilvie is written. Four hundred years have passed since St John's untimely death and martyrdom at Glasgow Cross on 10th March 1615. He died to defend the right of religious liberty during the highly charged period of the Scottish Reformation. At the tender age of thirteen, John Ogilvie was sent by his family from the shores of Leith to receive a thorough education in mainland Europe. He was a Scot of noble birth, born in 1579 into a highly respected Calvinist family; on his capture in Glasgow he informed his captors that his father was "Walter Ogilvie of Drum". His family background has therefore been associated with the wealthy laird, Sir Walter Ogilvie of Drum-na-Keith, in Strathisla, Banffshire. When John Ogilvie returned to his Scottish homeland after an absence of twenty-two years, he was an ordained priest of the Society of Jesus (SJ - the Jesuits).

Governed by faith and conscience he returned to Scotland to preach at a time of great religious upheaval, in a reformed Protestant Scotland. During this period, life for many Scots was overshadowed by intense suspicion and conflict. As a measure of safety and in order to preach the prohibited Mass in secret, Fr Ogilvie adopted the disguise of a horse dealer. But, sadly, the course of his Scottish ministry lasted

St John Ogilvie (1579-1615)

less than a year. He was betrayed and humiliated, suffered great brutality in prison, was put on trial for treason and hanged from the gallows for refusing to recognise the jurisdiction of the King. His final resting place was an unmarked grave, to ward off would-be pilgrims. Despite an ignominious death, John Ogilvie's influence endures. He is Scotland's only Catholic Reformation martyr. He was beatified in 1929 and canonised in 1976. His steadfast faith and courageous death reinforce the need to defend and uphold religious liberty as we mark the 400th anniversary of his martyrdom.

1. Discord and Reform

Scotland's Reformation Parliament signalled an unmitigated rupture with the papacy in 1560. The overall legacy of the Reformation is still hotly debated, but its escalation is often considered a vindication against the perceived faults and excesses of the Catholic Church, the Roman hierarchy and most notably, the papacy. It was a phenomenon which fundamentally altered the religious and political landscape of Scotland, culminating in the re-establishment of the Church along reformed lines. These changes included, amongst other things, the outright repudiation of the Pope's authority, the banning of the Catholic Mass and the promulgation of an approved Confession of Faith. Traditional analyses of the Reformation tend to view it as a single, momentous period in the history of the Church, highlighting key aspects of the Catholic-Protestant divide.

As a result, a host of uncompromising and partisan views have littered pages of Reformation historiography, and perceptions of the Scottish Reformation have been vulnerable to half-myths and distorted facts. But, thankfully, advances in rigorous scholarship, particularly since the 1950s, have shed light on conflicting interpretations in a more even-handed manner. In order to gain a clearer understanding of St John Ogilvie's life, we must be aware of the constraints and circumstances which shaped his priestly mission. Everyone's life has a context. Although we are shaped by our own agency, we are also influenced by the particulars of time and place: the period into which we are born, the people who are formative in our lives, and the environment in which we live. In an effort to be faithful to his spirit we must also try to perceive his life beyond the boundaries of our own modern-day perceptions.

In the first half of the sixteenth century there was a growing consciousness that church reform was long overdue. Reforming preachers such as Martin Luther (1483-1546) and humanist scholars such as Desiderius Erasmus (1466-1536) posed antagonistic questions about church practice and doctrine, with rumblings of Luther's "Ninety-five Theses" (a critique of the Church, especially the sale of indulgences) circulating in London as early as 1517. In Scotland, the sea ports of Ayr, Dundee and Leith were potential gateways for Lutheran and later Calvinist literature, although the extent to which this circulated is difficult to determine. Religious discontent in St Andrews was also galvanised by the brutal deaths of Protestant reformers Patrick Hamilton in 1528 and George Wishart in 1546, who were burned at the stake for heresy. Both men are considered important Protestant martyrs of the Scottish Reformation. Wishart was a confidant and mentor of John Knox (1514-1572), who became a fiery spokesman for reform in Scotland about a year after Wishart's death.

Although the year 1560 signifies its formal approval, the specific "birth" of the Scottish Reformation is inherently difficult to pin down. As a popular movement Protestantism had no deep roots in Scotland. Even among the reformers themselves there was a lack of agreement over the form and direction this alternative doctrine would take. During the fifteenth century, heresy (opinions at odds with the established religion) was generally confined to a small group and those who challenged the Church were inclined to flee from persecution to England and the continent. However, by the mid 1520s anti-heresy campaigns were established to quash a growing number of what were perceived as heretical notions. Heretics were considered traitors to the Church and, as such, traitors to God.

The established Church was increasingly criticised for corruption and superstition, including the trade in holy relics, the selling of indulgences, church involvement in secular issues, and the inability of churchmen to keep their vows or maintain their parishes. An important aspect of this criticism resulted from the practice of unjust papal taxation and inappropriate appointments to church posts. During the reign of James III of Scotland (1460-1488), a commendatory system (where secular rulers nominate men to ecclesiastical office) was introduced enabling the King to appoint lay abbots whose primary interest was the accumulation of wealth. Under this system, James V of Scotland (1513-1542) appointed five of his illegitimate sons to the richest abbeys in the country when they were still children. His only surviving legitimate child, Mary "Queen of Scots", succeeded him to the throne when she was just six days old. The secularisation of the Church was distinctly problematic, with the crown and nobility retaining much of its resources in thrall.

Other indicators of change were evident in higher levels of literacy among sections of the male population, following a decree by James IV (1488-1513) enabling landowners' sons to be educated. The invention of the printing press also promoted a wider dissemination of written materials, including William Tyndale's English translation of the bible during the 1530s. These evolving trends brought the word of God to a wider audience, breaking the monopoly on worship that the Church exercised through the liturgy, then normally in Latin. In addition, a renewed thirst for knowledge and lay spirituality formed a central component of the major cultural, social, economic and religious changes of the 14th and 15th century European Renaissance.

The bubonic plagues or "Black Death" during the 14th century had also had a devastating effect on ordinary clergy, who were open to infection when ministering to the sick. Many parishes were either without priests or filled by clergy who were untrained and unsuitable. Large numbers of clergy were also lost in long wars with England during the 13th and 14th centuries. Thus, the unity of medieval Christendom was seriously undermined by deep-rooted problems and external challenges that were difficult to control within the rigid structure of papal theocracy.

Despite growing insinuations against the Church there was evidence of self-criticism and calls for reform from influential Scottish clergy such as Ninian Winzet and Quentin Kennedy of Crossraguel, who were notable for their skill in argument while retaining a firm allegiance to Catholicism. Within a Scottish context some commentators suggest that the Counter-Reformation (the period of Catholic revival) pre-dates the Protestant Reformation of 1560, notably Archbishop Hamilton's reforming councils of 1549-1559.

All things considered, the Protestant Reformation gained momentum, in no small part, because seeds of reform from the Catholic Church failed to take sufficient root until the Council of Trent (1545-1563), when change in doctrine, discipline and devotion became more tangible. In 1562, the Jesuit Nicholas de Gouda arrived in Scotland as a papal envoy on a fact-finding mission, shortly after the reformed Church was established. But the role of both pre- and post-Reformation Jesuits in the preservation of the Catholic faith is worthy of greater consideration. It is often said that "in a crisis cleverness is born", and to be sure, a crisis in the ancient Church was brewing, but the root cause of the instability stemmed from a range of complex, unique and interrelated phenomena. The murky history of Church and State is a case in point, embodied in the political dynamics between Scotland, England and France.

2. Church and State

When King James V of Scotland (1513-42) married French-born Mary of Guise in 1538 it reinforced support for Catholicism and the "auld alliance" of 1295, when Scotland and France signed a Treaty of Friendship and mutual support against England, their common adversary. King Henry VIII of England (1491-1547), laid the foundation for the English reformation by rejecting the spiritual jurisdiction of the Pope who disagreed with his decision to divorce Catherine of Aragon (considered too old to produce a male heir for Henry, who wanted to marry his mistress Anne Boleyn). Consequently, Henry renounced Catholicism and induced Parliament to make him head of the Church in England; he dissolved the monasteries, drove out the monks and confiscated land to the benefit of his supporters. To prevent Scotland supporting France in a war against England, Henry's army marched north and defeated the Scots at Solway Moss in 1542. In the same year, Mary "Queen of Scots" was born at Linlithgow Palace. Her father, James V of Scotland, died when she was only six days old and she became queen, with her mother, Mary of Guise, acting as regent.

Hoping to disrupt an alliance between Scotland and France, Henry commended that Mary and his infant son

Edward be married. To his fury, Scots nobles (fearing an English takeover) would not consent to this arrangement and Henry retaliated with the so-called "Rough Wooing" (1544-1551), a series of mostly unsuccessful, brutal attacks on Scotland. At the age of five Mary was packed off to France for safe-keeping, where she was betrothed to four-year-old François, heir to the throne of France. The young couple were married in magnificent splendour in the cathedral of Notre Dame, Paris in 1558. In 1559, Mary's husband was crowned François II, making Mary his queen consort. However their reign was cut short when the sickly François died aged sixteen, the year after he ascended to the throne, leaving Mary an inconsolable widow at eighteen.

The Queen Regent of Scotland, Mary of Guise, was a formidable defender of the "auld alliance" until her death in 1560, when French troops left Scotland. In the same year, an Act of the Scottish Parliament put an end to the Pope's authority, establishing Scotland as a Protestant country. From this time, Protestant England was an ally of Scotland and the Reformation in Scotland and England was staunchly supported under the rule of Queen Elizabeth I (1558-1603). In 1561, a resplendent Mary Queen of Scots stepped ashore in Leith after an absence of thirteen years. She was to begin her rule of Protestant Scotland following the deaths of her mother, her father-in-law Henry II of France (1519-1559) and her young husband, François II.

Faced with enormous challenges, Mary accepted the Protestant-led government with cautious moderation. Her rule as a Catholic was inherently fragile, due to the threat of rebellion by Protestant noblemen. At twenty-two she married her cousin, Henry Stewart, Lord Darnley (1545-1567), a man whose jealously and drunkenness exceeded his superficial charm. Although disastrous in many ways, the marriage did produce a much-desired heir. Their son, James, was born in Edinburgh Castle on 19th June 1566 and baptised a Catholic at Stirling Castle. However, a dark shadow hung over Mary due to Darnley's involvement in the death of her personal secretary David Rizzio, shortly before her son's birth.

Events then turned from bad to worse after Darnley was murdered at Kirk o' Field in 1567. Then, under bizarre circumstances, Mary was abducted by a powerful Scottish nobleman, the Earl of Bothwell, who became her third husband. Suspicions of Bothwell's involvement in Darnley's murder outraged many of Mary's subjects who subsequently turned against her. In 1567, she was compelled to abdicate in favour of her infant son, James (aged thirteen months), who was crowned King of Scots at the Church of the Holy Rude, Stirling. John Knox preached at the coronation and James was raised as a member of the Protestant Church.

After attempts to restore her rights as queen were defeated, Mary fled to England, seeking help from her rival and cousin Elizabeth I. However, the "tragic queen" was imprisoned in a variety of houses and castles for nineteen years, put on trial over the "casket letters" and found guilty of taking part in a plot to kill Elizabeth. Mary was beheaded at Fortheringhay Castle on 8th February 1587. As yet, the precise identity of Darnley's murderer is still unknown and grounds for Mary's alleged complicity are unresolved. Her only son was to become James VI King of Scotland, and James I King of England following the death of the childless Elizabeth in 1603. This same King would have an important role in the fate of Fr John Ogilvie during his captivity in Glasgow and Edinburgh: the "Jesuit in disguise", who returned to Scotland to "un-teach heresy".

3. A Life Apart

Although much of John Ogilvie's early life remains hidden and obscure, we can say with a degree of certainty that he was born on or very close to the year 1579. His upbringing was in the reformed Calvinist faith (later known as Presbyterianism); as we have seen, Scotland had embarked on the rocky road to Reformation around twenty years beforehand. In 1592, when John Ogilvie was thirteen years old, he was sent by his family to Europe to broaden his education. Some might say he was just a boy, but by sixteenth century standards this practice was not uncommon. As far as we know, there are no genealogical records verifying John Ogilvie's parentage. However, during his captivity Ogilvie stated he was born in the north of Scotland, and that he was the firstborn son of Walter Ogilvie of Drum. This is sometimes referred to as Drum-na-Keith due to its proximity to the small town of Keith, in the Scottish county of Banffshire.

John Ogilvie also identified himself as belonging to this area on entering the Jesuit order in 1599, when he was twenty years old. His father has therefore been identified with the wealthy Scottish landowner, Sir Walter Ogilvie of Findlater, on the grounds that Sir Walter's property included the land of Drum-na-Keith. If this account of his ancestry is true, John Ogilvie would have had the right of inheritance in one of the most influential families in the north-east of Scotland. His mother would have been Lady Agnes Elphinstone (whose brother George entered the Society of Jesus shortly after John's birth in 1579). In 1582 Walter Ogilvie remarried following the death of his first wife. Thus their firstborn son would have had a new stepmother named Lady Mary Douglas "of Lochleven". The infant John would have been no more than three years old at the time of his mother's death.

At the time of his trial John Ogilvie stated, "They ask me if I am of noble birth. I say that I am and so were my parents before me." Walter Ogilvie's father, James, had been treasurer to Mary Queen of Scots and there are claims that the family tree can be traced back to William, King of Scotland, and Queen Margaret. Pride in his Scottish ancestry was also evident with his reference to King James VI of Scotland and I of England: "I am as much a subject as he". Within months of John Ogilvie's death in 1615, Walter Ogilvie was granted the peerage of Lord Ogilvie of Dexford; his son James succeeded to the peerage in 1625 and was later appointed Earl of Findlater in 1638. It is very probable that Walter Ogilvie's Calvinist position would have been helpful to the family in obtaining for their son the government permit required for travelling abroad. This policy was enforced to guard against unwanted Catholic influence and to deter Catholics from developing their faith outside their own country.

4. Prayer of the Heart

In 1592, the year John Ogilvie left his native home, a Scot of this name matriculated at the Protestant University of Helmstedt, located in northern Germany. Little is known about the early years of our subject's experience abroad, except that he became immersed in the intense religious debate which held sway throughout the continent. In the midst of the intellectual and theological climate of post-Reformation Europe, it is natural to wonder how John Ogilvie's conversion from Calvinism to Catholicism came about. Some insights may be gleaned from extracts from his trial, when he addressed the Lords of the Privy Council. These reports, written in Scotland and later compiled in Italian, were possibly put together by Fr Patrick Anderson, the Rector at the Scots College in Rome, who was an associate of John Ogilvie in France:

> He begged the Lords of the Council to remember that he had been brought up in Scotland to believe Calvinism to be the true religion, but that, being guided by God to leave his own country for a time to go abroad, he had chanced to consult various learned men in Italy, France and Germany as to the true faith and religion. In consequence thereof his soul had become sick with

anxiety and interior doubts concerning this matter for he could not tell which, amongst the great varieties of religious bodies he saw in Europe, was the true one, and he resolved at least to leave the matter to God, for the disputes rendered the subject daily more complicated and perplexed. In taking this step he had relied on those texts of the Sacred Scriptures which tell us: "God wishes all men to be saved and to come to an acknowledgement of his truth", and "Come to me all ye that labour and are burdened and I will refresh you".

After long deliberation, he had come to see that every probability and rational motive led to a reception of the Catholic religion. There were to be found numbers of all classes, emperors, kings, princes, and many other noblemen; there was the unity of the faith which had ever been most marked in the Roman Church; antiquity, unbroken succession, sincere and perfect virtue shown in rejecting the world and shown by its members of every rank and class. A multitude of miracles wrought in testimony of the Roman faith, a multitude of very learned men who had defended and still did daily defend the Roman faith, and in these last times there were unnumbered hosts of holy martyrs who had died in its defence. On the other hand, he had realised that the Scottish ministers could not claim for their religion either antiquity or succession; they could not bring evidence either of miracles or unity; nor could they urge its reception for motives worthy of a wise man nor by appeal to their Bible, which was indeed on many counts far different from the true text.

There is truth in the divine paradox that with loss of self we can find God more clearly. Scripture also tells us that "God dwells within us" (*1 Co* 3:16). Whatever soul-searching took place, John Ogilvie followed the prompting of grace and registered as a student at the Catholic Scots College of Douai, France in 1596. It was also here that his Calvinist background was confirmed. Fr Crichton, the then Rector of Scots College, compiled a register of students at the close of his term of office in 1598. Under the date 1596 it was noted that *Joannes Ogilby ex Calviniano factus Catholicus* - John Ogilvie, previously a Calvinist, was now converted to Catholicism. However, recurrent financial constraints at Douai led to the transfer of students to Louvain near Brussels.

In June 1598 records indicate that John Ogilvie was sent to the Scottish Benedictine abbey at Regensburg (sometimes referred to by its English name, Ratisbon) in Bavaria, although there is no record of his actual arrival. However, by the end of 1598 he was studying at the Jesuit seminary of Olmutz in Moravia, a state in central Europe (modern-day Czech Republic). It is plausible that John Ogilvie's decision to apply for admission into the Society of Jesus was reached at Olmutz. In the meantime an outbreak of the plague delayed the Jesuit Provincial's visit to the seminary, which in turn delayed John Ogilvie's application to join the Jesuits. But in this situation we can catch a glimpse of John Ogilvie's independent spirit as, undeterred, he made his own way to Vienna to ask permission to join the Society. Thus on 5th November 1599 he entered the Jesuit Austrian-Bohemian province novitiate at Brunn (Brno) in earnest preparation to train as a Jesuit.

The noviceship house at Brunn is noted for its association with Edmund Campion (1540-1581) who died a horrific martyrdom for his part in the English Jesuit mission. Campion's letters from Prague in 1575 were held in reverence by incoming novices, amongst whom was John Ogilvie. After studying Philosophy for three years at Graz (south-east Austria) John Ogilvie taught for around two years at Vienna. There then followed a year's study of apologetics (essentially a reasoned defence of what you believe in), then a further two years at Olmutz, leading to his final vows as a Jesuit on 26th December 1601.

As well as the traditional vows of poverty, chastity and obedience, he took (like all Jesuits) an additional vow of obedience to the Pope with respect to mission. Ignatius Loyola (1491-1556), the founder of the Society of Jesus, was a Spanish soldier who experienced a spiritual conversion during a period of recuperation from a serious military injury. Ignatius believed that the most reliable way to finding God's will was through the person who held the greatest universal responsibility - their Religious Superior in Rome. During the leadership of Claudio Aquaviva (1581-1615) the Society's membership expanded with a concomitant rise in colleges, churches and missions. Then as now, the Jesuits would strive for exemplary scholarly and spiritual credentials with training lasting as long as between eight and fourteen years (depending on previous background and educational experience). Their ministry focused on preaching and catechising, coupled with Loyola's *Spiritual Exercises* (meditation and contemplations which helped instil inner conversion, discernment and a lifelong commitment to Jesus). Although there are no definitive records, it is generally accepted that John Ogilvie was ordained a priest of the Society of Jesus in 1610, when he was sent by his Jesuit-General to Paris in the company of Fr George Elphinstone (recognised in a range of sources as his uncle, his mother's brother). Shortly afterwards, he was posted as a confessor to students in Rouen, north-west France, where Joan of Arc was executed for heresy in 1431 and where exiled priests gave grim accounts of persecuted Catholics in Scotland.

From this point onwards, Fr Ogilvie urged his superior, Fr Gordon "of Huntly", to allow him to work in the dangerous mission work of Scotland. From their first mission to Ireland and Scotland in the early 1540s, Jesuits played an important role in safeguarding the Catholic faith in Scotland. The early Jesuits, such as William Murdoch, William Crichton, James Gordon and Edmund Hay were well accustomed to pre-Reformation Scotland. Robert Abercromby was also recognised for his part in the conversion of Queen Anne of Denmark, the wife of King James VI of Scotland and James I of England.

Despite the unfaltering efforts of Jesuits for greater tolerance towards Catholics, James VI was a skilled political philosopher who would play one group off against another. Although he desired to be a "universal king", he engaged in heated theological controversy with the learned Jesuits Robert Bellarmine and Francisco Suarez over his "Divine Right" basis for monarchy. Books from both Jesuits were conspicuous at Fr Ogilvie's final trial. The King's introduction of Episcopalian bishops, responsible only to him, also enraged Presbyterians who despised any notion of Episcopal hierarchy, so, to relieve their fears, the grip on Catholics tightened. There were also fearful rumours about Spanish rule in Scotland and the scandal of the Gunpowder Plot of 1605. One year later, the controversial "Oath of Allegiance" was introduced. This act defined as treason the refusal of subjects to recognise the monarch's supremacy in spiritual as well as temporal matters. In essence, the Oath would deny the Pope's authority over the King. Thus Catholics were greatly oppressed with severe laws against them, and threats of fines, eviction, banishment or death itself, if they persisted in fidelity to their faith.

For ordinary Catholics, their faith was traditionally expressed through attendance at Mass, devotion to the

Rosary, prayers to the Saints, to Mary the Mother of God and to Jesus (particularly the passion of Jesus). Religious imagery, such as paintings, statues, crucifixes, and stained glass, helped to give meaning and form to central aspects of the Catholic faith. It is also arguable that as most ordinary Scots were illiterate, religious symbolism played a vital role in enhancing and instructing lay faith. However, John Knox and other Scottish Protestant reformers rallied vehemently against "superstitious" practices and "idolatry", which included the Mass:

> that abominable ydoll the mess as ane of the maist devillisch and superstitious inventioun of the antichrist.

The "three notes" identified in the Confession of Faith regarding the "true Kirk of God" according to the Reformers were "the true preaching of the word of God", "the right administration of the sacraments of Christ Jesus" and "ecclesiastical discipline uprightly ministered". But it is worth pressing the point that, for many laypeople, criticism of the Church did not automatically make someone a Protestant, nor was his or her traditional faith in God irreversibly diminished or changed overnight.

In a letter to the General of the Jesuits, the Earl of Angus stressed the difficulties of the Scottish mission and the need for Jesuit fathers: "I entreat Your Reverence, to send none but such as both desire, and are able to bear with a courageous heart the burden and heat of the day".

In fact two experienced Jesuits, Frs Robert Abercromby and Patrick Anderson, were compelled to leave Scotland. After an agonising period of deliberation regarding the best approach to "take into consideration the affairs of Scotland", Jesuit General Claudio Acquaviva eventually gave his consent for Fr Ogilvie to return to his native land. Following a lengthy absence of twenty-two years he would go back to the land of his birth and begin a mission exclusively focused on a post-Reformation Scotland. In November 1613 Fr Ogilvie once again breathed the cold air of Leith harbour. He was joined on the journey by fellow Jesuit James Moffat and Fr John Campbell, a Capuchin.

The journey itself was hazardous as ports across Britain were full of spies, with watchful eyes and listening ears. Anti-Catholic laws were well established, having now been in force for over fifty years. On arrival in Scotland the men parted quickly, clothed in secular disguise. Fr Campbell went to Edinburgh, Fr Moffat to the Lowlands and Fr Ogilvie to the north of Scotland. When John Ogilvie first left Scotland he was a young boy uncertain of his way in the world. He now returned as a Jesuit priest with ambitions that absorbed his entire life, namely the reconciliation of people to the Catholic faith. For safety, he assumed the name John Watson, a former soldier, now seeking his living as a horse dealer.

5. A Jesuit in Disguise

Records of Fr Ogilvie's movements over the next few months are patchy, but accounts taken from his own written testimony and those of his close companions help to establish a general outline. He spent part of the winter of 1613 in the north of Scotland, most likely at Strathbogie, where clandestine Catholics such as the Earl of the Huntly resided, before travelling back to Edinburgh in the new year of 1614. In preparation for the Scottish mission he was given a list of names of Catholics who provided support and shelter to adherents of the faith, including mission priests. Consequently, Fr Ogilvie was welcomed by William Sinclair and his family who lived in the Canongate area of the capital. Sinclair was a young advocate and a convert to Catholicism, who proved to be a very faithful and courageous friend. To harbour a priest could result in death or exile (in due course, Sinclair was sentenced to death, but later was banished from Scotland). Fr Ogilvie also managed to infiltrate Edinburgh Castle, where his kindness and humanity were a ray of hope for Sir James MacDonald, who languished in prison there on account of his faith.

Then, around three months later, there was a mysterious trip to London. Whatever the cause, it involved King James or his ministers. Most likely, the trip was an endeavour to secure greater leniency for the King's Catholic subjects. From London, Fr Ogilvie made his way to Paris and by the end of March he was face to face with a rather exasperated superior. Fr Huntly was experienced enough to know that "word of mouth" pledges from the royal court were worthless, and in the beginning of April, a crestfallen Fr Ogilvie was ordered back to Scotland to continue his mission. In June he moved westward towards Renfrewshire, where some noble families remained secret Catholics. Authoritative sources suggest that, following this visit to the south-west of Glasgow, the young laird Hugh Sempill of Craigbet (who had taken the obligatory Protestant oath on matriculating at Glasgow University) later sold his property to travel abroad and train as a Jesuit.

In Scotland, Fr Ogilvie ministered secretly and divided his time largely between Glasgow and Edinburgh. He administered the sacraments, reconciled those who had lapsed and tried to make new converts whenever possible. Mass was often held in the Glasgow home of Marion Walker, a spirited elderly widow, who had been hauled up before Kirk elders a decade earlier for "idolatry". When asked why she kept a crucifix in her house, she had indignantly replied that she would "have mair of them if [she] had the silver!" Another associate called Robert Heygate kept a stationer's shop on Glasgow High Street; he helped to inform Catholics in the community about celebrations of Mass. A touching letter (below) from Fr Ogilvie to Fr Alber, Jesuit

Provincial of Austria, during the summer of 1614 gives an important insight into the everyday aspect of his mission. The hazardous nature and demands of the mission are stressed along with a heartfelt plea for support for another Jesuit, Fr Crichton, who was at risk of further captivity.

The harvest here is very great and the labourers very few. One of them Fr Andrew Crichton, the bearer of this letter, who previously spent a long time in chains for the faith, is now leaving his country, lest he falls a second time into the enemy's hands. As he is too well known by reason of his earlier imprisonment, he would bring into danger the gentlemen with whom he would be forced to stay and who would be very afraid to receive him into their houses and conceal him there. So if there is any matter in which he needs your Reverence's help or your fatherly advice, I beg your Reverence to show him paternal charity. He deserves every attention that Christian kindness can bestow because of the hardships he has suffered and the great good he has done in this most remote region of earth. For myself, I am known to nobody and I am engaged day and night in more work than I can cope with in any day. My companion is in hiding, and wisely, for there are many persons here who knew him in Italy and have no love of the Church of God. God be praised - by day I go freely about my business in the market place, and at night, I can carry out without suspicion the duties of my vocation. I commend myself to your prayers.

Your Reverence's servant in Christ and unworthy son, John Ogilvie. Edinburgh, 26-27th July 1614.

Within a few months Fr Ogilvie's letters would be written from a prison cell. After the martyr's death, depositions (testimonies under oath) confirmed he celebrated a number of Masses and reconciled various people to the faith. As stated in the testimony of one of his closest associates, William Sinclair:

He lost no chance or opportunity in spreading the Faith. He entered prisons, at very great risk to his own life. In all these actions he displayed such earnestness, keenness and ardour, that I could infer that his heart burned with a most fervent desire for spreading the faith.

This desire for spreading the faith was the reason Fr Ogilvie returned to Glasgow from Edinburgh in early October 1614. There were five people interested in being reconciled - but one of them could not be trusted.

6. The Informer Proves his Worth

Around four o'clock in the afternoon on Tuesday 4th
October 1614, Fr Ogilvie walked towards the Market
Square in Glasgow. His glance was clear and his movement
robust. He was on his way to meet a man who sought
instruction in the faith, identified in a range of sources as
"Adam Boyd". In Fr Ogilvie's own testimony, titled *Relatio
Incarcerationis* (*An Account of My Imprisonment*), written
"furtively and hurriedly" and smuggled out by wives and
friends of other prisoners, we are given a poignant account
of his betrayal, imprisonment and trial shortly before his
death. With respect to the informer:

> I was betrayed by one of those whom I had to receive
> back to the Church, a man of very good family, and
> of great wealth who had been recommended to me by
> many as a Catholic, and as one who for a long time had
> been on the lookout for some opportunity of reception.

En route, Fr Ogilvie was walking with an acquaintance
in the square. Various sources name this man as "James
Stewart", son of the former Lord Provost of Glasgow. But
a trap had been set and following a covert signal, a servant
of the Archbishop advanced towards the unsuspecting
Jesuit with an order to follow him to "his lordship". The

exchange also produced an impression on passers-by and glances of distrust and suspicion developed amongst those assembled in the Market Square. Overhearing the command, Fr Ogilvie's companion grew concerned and forcefully questioned the authority of the order, but the mood in the crowd turned ugly. Fr Ogilvie, who tried to restore calm, was assailed with blows. His cloak was stolen (although later retrieved) and he was physically dragged to the house of Lord Provost James Hamilton.

On hearing of the fracas, Glasgow Archbishop John Spottiswoode, a man of renown and action, made his way towards Hamilton's house, accompanied by a group of gentry and an armed guard. As Spottiswoode walked towards him, Fr Ogilvie rose to his feet, to be met by a stunning blow to his face and an authoritative reprimand: "You are bold to say your Masses in a reformed city". The chastisement was fierce and disproportionate. Reeling from the blow but with forceful indignation Fr Ogilvie answered, "You act like a hangman and not a bishop in striking me." This reply proved to be prophetic.

His reply to the Archbishop prompted an additional assault: "they rained blows on me, they tore my hair and my beard, and they scratched my face with their nails". Fr Ogilvie was then forced to strip and his personal possessions were taken. These included his breviary; a book of religious doctrine; a small amount of money; a silver reliquary (which contained holy relics of St Ignatius, St Margaret of

Scotland and St Catherine); a ring; a seal used for letters; and some medicinal powder. The next day his horse was taken from the inn and his room was ransacked. In his own testimony Fr Ogilvie related that other goods were seized including "altar furniture, Fr Patrick's letters about our property in Scotland and Fr Murdoch's list of names". It is also feasible that the names of others associated with the Jesuit were disclosed by the informer. The lodgings were apparently "betrayed by a Frenchman", despite the view that "it was safe enough had men kept faith and silence". But there are always those who, unobserved, observe everything. The scene, as outlined above, marks a decisive turning point in Fr Ogilvie's short life. On Tuesday 4th October, his day began with an ardent desire to advance his Jesuit vocation but it ended in his betrayal and loss of liberty. Prior to the treachery in the Market Square, Tuesday morning also marked the celebration of his final Mass.

The Burgh Court of Glasgow, October 1614

The next day, 5th October, the captured Jesuit was brought from prison to the Bishop's Hall bearing the marks of aggression from the day before. He was weak from hunger and his frame was chilled from his freezing cell. The silence was broken by the Archbishop of Glasgow who led the proceedings, observed by a great concourse of "lairds and preachers". Two members of the Privy Council were

John Spottiswoode (1565-1639) Archbishop of Glasgow
during the captivity of John Ogilvie (SJ)

also summoned. The focus centred on three main themes within a range of lengthy, often repetitive questions.

"Have you said Mass in the King's dominions?" was the first main question. Although saying Mass was considered a treasonable act, the Catholic Church questioned the right of a temporal authority to legislate in spiritual matters. Accordingly, Fr Ogilvie replied: "As no law binds me, I will swear to answer when I see fit." He also refused on the common law ground that no accused was obliged to incriminate himself or others (those associated with his mission). Following similar questions, and contrary to expectation (and to his questioners' annoyance), he candidly stressed he would not say anything in "prejudice of myself or an innocent neighbour".

They asked, "Do you acknowledge the King?" He replied: "James is the *de facto* King of Scotland." Ogilvie later admitted, "At this point I was very frightened; but the fools, not having learned the technical phrases of the law, did not know how to continue the examination."

Thirdly, the court declared it to be a crime of treason "to assert that the Pope has spiritual jurisdiction in the King's dominions". Fr Ogilvie answered, "it is of faith to hold that." This referred to the authority given directly by Jesus to Peter, the first Vicar of Christ, to take care of his Church - "feed my lambs". He continued, "Judges such as they are should hunt down crime and not sacrifices. Thefts, treachery, murders, these belong to the King's forum, but the sacraments of religion do not." The court replied, "Do you dare to put your signature to that?" He answered, "Even with my blood if need be." Thus Fr Ogilvie denied that this was treason. Indeed, in the course of the questioning, he raised an issue which nettled many of those present. As Protestant Scotland was shifting uncomfortably between Episcopalianism and Presbyterianism, he highlighted the "treasonable" behaviour of some ministers and their Protestant followers who maintained an allegiance to "God and Kirk" rather than "God and King".

After twenty-six hours without food, and shaking from fever, he was allowed a short time to sit by the fire; but his repose was disturbed by a highlander who rebuked him for fraudulently claiming the noble name of "Ogilvie". The highlander declared, "if it was not for respect of the noblemen present I would throw you into the burning fire." Without anger or rancour Fr Ogilvie jokingly replied, "It could never happen more conveniently than now for I am very cold, but take care, lest I scatter the cinders and coals through the house, as you might be compelled to sweep them up". With these and similar jokes he responded to taunts, and when the truth of his nobility was verified, the highlander promised to do anything for him. When the hearing eventually concluded, Fr Ogilvie returned to his miserable cell. He was later fastened with two rings to an iron bar weighing about two hundred pounds, which considerably restricted his movements, but not his prayers.

Meanwhile, the authorities rounded up and arrested those who had attended his Masses, including old Marion whose house was used as a Mass centre. She never saw her home again and died under house arrest in another location prior to Fr Ogilvie's execution.

During the next five months Fr Ogilvie was examined at least five times. From October 1614 to March 1615 many men of "high standing" formed part of the proceedings. But the key players were Archbishop John Spottiswoode, the Presbyterian minister turned Archbishop, and John Ogilvie, a Calvinist boy turned Jesuit Priest. Following two months of captivity in Glasgow, Fr Ogilvie was taken to Edinburgh, prompted by a letter from Archbishop Spottiswoode to King James. Spottiswoode suggested that if answers to questions were not forthcoming then the use of "the boots" or other persuasions should be applied so that the names and homes of Catholics might be revealed. "The boots" were a form of medieval torture that caused excruciating pain by tightening iron plates around the feet, to lacerate the flesh and crush the bones of the victim.

Edinburgh, December 1614

It was December, in the cold of winter, when the prisoner, escorted by guards, left Glasgow for Edinburgh. The King's letter had arrived to confirm that the Jesuit should be examined there. Outside in the courtyard angry taunts became audible as a hostile crowd waited for his departure.

He was put on horseback, with powerless hands secured behind his back, and could do little to prevent the onslaught of "mud, snow and curses" from the crowd. Such was his character that he said in jest, "it's past joking when the heid's aff." Then above the crowd a woman shrieked, "A curse on your ugly face." It was Elizabeth Heygate, Robert Heygate's desperate mother. Fr Ogilvie replied, "Christ's blessings on your bonny face." There was something noble in his sentiment and she soon regretted her menacing words: "She openly proclaimed her sorrow for what she said and promised never again to speak evil of me". However, it must be acknowledged that Fr Ogilvie was greatly pained by accusations and rumours that he had betrayed the names of Catholics now held in prison by the authorities. Nothing was further from the truth. Gradually, many would gain a fresh understanding of him and respect his integrity, lively wit and intelligence, and his deep love for Christ and his neighbour. "The heretics noticed how I returned blessings for curses and was good-humoured to those who were raging at me."

In Edinburgh on 12th December, Fr Ogilvie was presented before the Lords Commissioners appointed by the King. He was subjected to a raft of interrogations. Points raised in Glasgow were reiterated before the interrogators moved specifically to questions about those people he had contacted during his mission. Again the questions rained down: "Who harboured you?" "Who did you reconcile to the Catholic faith?" But he would not incriminate others, for by betraying his neighbour he would "offend God and kill his own soul".

They said: "You ought not to have come into this realm against the King's commands." He replied: "The King cannot forbid me my country without legitimate reason, for that same natural law which makes him King makes me a subject." They then raised the question of the Mass: "The King forbids Masses, and you say them". He replied: "Judge ye whether I ought rather to obey Christ or the King. For Christ (Luke xxii) instituted the Mass and ordered it to be offered up, as I will prove if you want me to. If then, the King condemns that which Christ has instituted, how will he escape the name of persecutor?"

The Vigil

It grew dark and they eventually gave up. But much thought was given to their next tactic with the Jesuit. He was to endure a torture called an enforced "vigil". According to Fr Ogilvie's own account, "for eight days and nine complete nights they forced me to stay awake, using sharp pointed rods, pins, needles, and blows". Four of Spottiswoode's men were assigned to take shifts to impose the vigil day and night. When exhaustion made Fr Ogilvie numb to stabs and blows, he was raised to full height and dropped, crashing senseless to the ground. Many witnessed this ordeal and, Fr Ogilvie later noted, "news of it spread the length and breadth of Scotland, so that many were angered and pitied my sufferings." Doctors recorded his demise, saying he had three hours to live. His senses were dulled, his face haggard, his clear, intelligent eyes were sunk in his head and his limbs ached. He was more dead than alive. At last they left him to his troubled slumber.

On the tenth day, 22nd December, the Lords of the Council recalled the shattered and exhausted Jesuit - "I scarce knew where I was". They spoke of their leniency in applying sleeplessness rather than "the boots". The questions resumed, including the warning, "unless you do the King's will, worse will follow". Summoning up his strength he pointedly addressed them:

> You try to convert me and you seek a conversion after the heart of your ministers, the conversion of a rational man into a madman, a Jesuit into a fool. You can keep your fat living if it is to be obtained by a conversion like that.

He stressed, "I will not add to nor alter anything that I have said. I trust not in myself but in God's grace. I ask no mercy. Only one thing I ask, that what you do, you do quickly." The Archbishop advised him he was speaking in passion, adding, "No one wants to die quickly when he can save his life…as you can if you take the rewards offered to you with the King's favour." Those words had a decisive effect and he replied;

No, I am not speaking in passion, but deliberately and I shall preserve my life if I may…only I am not obliged to lose God in so doing. But since I can't keep both life and God, I willingly lose the lesser for the greater good.

Glasgow, Christmas 1614

On 23rd December Archbishop Spottiswoode began the long journey back to Glasgow with his weary prisoner, arriving back on Christmas Eve. It was noted later by Fr Ogilvie that the Archbishop had shown him friendship when they reached Glasgow: "He (Spottiswoode) talks to me in a most friendly way". Indeed, for a short period, conditions were somewhat more liberal; an iron collar was fastened around just one ankle, mainly to prevent disease from lying on his back. He was also allowed pen and paper to prepare his forthcoming defence. As noted previously, some of this material was used to record a discreet testimony of his captivity. Sheets of paper were slipped out under his door and passed by visitors to other Catholic prisoners. Meanwhile, in London, the inscrutable King James was also writing. He was a monarch who took great pride in his passion for theological controversy, as reflected in a carefully drawn-up list of five questions for the final trial of the Jesuit. In mid January, Fr Ogilvie responded in writing to the King's questions. Needless to say, their contrasting positions would be not reconciled.

As the weeks passed, relations between the Archbishop

and his prisoner seemed to cool. Visits from the Archbishop's wife, suggesting a sneaking sympathy for the Jesuit, were brought to an abrupt end by her irate husband. The resident gaoler who had developed a liking for his prisoner was also replaced by the Archbishop's own steward, a hard-faced, hard-hearted man, who reinforced Ogilvie's chains and left him to languish in solitude, under heavy surveillance. These altered circumstances were noticed by other prisoners and are apparent in the tone of his letters from this time. The first was written out of concern for John Mayne, a young university graduate who took the Protestant Oath at Glasgow University but later became a Catholic. He was arrested for hearing Mass and held in prison at the same time as Fr Ogilvie:

'I John Ogilvie, Priest of the Society of Jesus, was arrested three months ago for faith's sake and the bearer of this letter John Mayne, M.A. was arrested with me. I lie now in prison at Glasgow burdened with weights of 100 lbs or more: I await death. I am witness that the aforesaid bearer of this letter has suffered much in prison, has lost his country and his property because he remained firm in the true faith. By the judge's sentence he is outlawed and condemned to die if he remains in Scotland. Wherefore, if the King's shame should change this sentence into exile, let Catholics be mindful of Christian charity, lest the means of life be lacking to one who, for Christ's sake, has heard the judge condemn him to death. Written hurriedly and secretly in my cell at Glasgow, 28th Jan. 1615.'

The letter below, which incorporates a covering letter for Fr Alber, the Provincial of the Jesuits, is possibly the last letter written by Fr Ogilvie. Its motivation, once again, is support for his fellow prisoner, John Mayne. One can also detect his comprehension that death will follow soon:

You will learn best from John Mayne, the bearer of this letter, how I am situated. It is a serious crime to be discovered writing, so I must make haste before the gaoler returns. Your reverence received me into the Society of Jesus in Austria, and on this account I commend my children to you (as to a grandfather) with greater confidence; I hope therefore that if John Mayne, the bearer of this letter, should need your help he will find the most worthy Ferdinand to be a veritable father of German charity.

A part of my experiences I have written and sent to Mr Mayne. Let him have them prepared for the annals if you like, and along with them anything he shall have done. I commend me to your prayers. Written from Glasgow prison, in which I am loaded with a 200lb iron weight, and where I look forward to death unless I accept the King's gifts, a fat living, and abjure my faith. I was tortured once by a vigil of 9 nights and 8 days;

now I await the second torture and - after death…The gaoler will come. (Dated 22nd February).

Shortly afterwards, the King's messenger brought royal letters which confirmed the Jesuit would be condemned for treason if he insisted on adhering to his answers to the King's questions. The magistrates also confirmed the formal date of the trial, which was set for the last day of February. In Scotland the Old Style calendar was used until 1752; the New Style or Gregorian calendar (used on the Continent) would record the trial as 10th March 1615. William Sinclair's deposition to the 1629 Commission in Rome (an official inquiry in a cause of canonisation) cited Fr Ogilvie's death on 10th March. Archbishop John Spottiswoode's recording of the same event was recorded as 28th February 1615 - a difference of 10 days. Obviously the use of different calendars to document facts can result in confusion, but it is more important that the evidence is intact.

7. The King's Jurisdiction

On Tuesday 10th March 1615, Fr Ogilvie was taken from his prison in the Bishop's palace in Glasgow to the Tollbooth on the High Street. He had to face a special commission appointed by the King, a jury of fifteen "discreet and substantial persons" headed, naturally, by Spottiswoode. On the day before his final trial, his feet were washed. That evening his prayers were disturbed by the construction of the scaffold, in preparation for execution. When he faced the refined dignitaries he wore an ill-fitting, short coat that was torn under the arm. His gaoler, the one inclined to use force without pity, appropriated his "good" coat. What need would the Jesuit have for it? The jury focused on the claims of the papacy rather than "Mass and converting citizens", which added a new shade to the proceedings.

The questioning continued along the following lines: Could the Pope be judge and have spiritual powers over his majesty? Does he have power to excommunicate kings, particularly if they are not of his Church? Does he have the power to depose or slay kings? And finally, does the Pope have the authority to absolve subjects from the oath of allegiance to his majesty?

These questions were carefully framed to elicit either an acceptance or a rejection of the claim of the "divine right" of

En tibi, Rex, supra, cum Pallade doctus Apollo,
    In laudes merito, Magne Iacobe, tuas:
Infra te posita est Pax alma et Copia rerum,
    Quam felix populus, Magne Iacobe, tuus!

King James VI of Scotland and James I of England (1566-1623)

the King in matters spiritual and temporal. Thus, regarding the question of excommunication, it was acknowledged as an established doctrine of the Church that the Pope could impose sanctions. To all the other questions, Fr Ogilvie claimed no spiritual jurisdiction, as these were a matter for the Pope. Finally he condemned the Oath of Supremacy and the Oath of Allegiance and stressed:

> I deny any point made against me as treason, for if it were treason it would be treason in all places and in all kingdoms but that is not known to be so. As for your acts of Parliament; they are made by a number of partial men, the best of the land not agreeing with them and of matters not subject to their forum or judicatory, for which I will not give a rotten fig.

They answered, "But are you not willing to comply with the King's will?" In the course of this and other interrogations, Fr Ogilvie clearly stated his temporal duty to the King: "In every duty, which I owe the King's majesty I will show myself a most obedient subject; for if any invade his temporal rights I would shed my last drop of blood in his defence".

In Scotland, the Parliament of 1606 had passed the Sovereignty Act 1606. Here was a "sovereign monarch, absolute prince, judge and governor over all persons, estates and causes, both spiritual and temporal". Such was the context of Fr Ogilvie's trial. To deny the King's authority was considered treasonable. Yet to assert the King's authority in spiritual matters was for Catholics (and for Presbyterians who loathed the authority of bishops) irreconcilable with the Church's mission.

With such questions raised and answered, Fr Ogilvie's fate was inevitable. The jury left to consider their verdict. Following their deliberations, he was convicted of treason, as defined by law. He was to be taken to the gallows and hanged. He would then be beheaded, his body quartered and exposed for public view. With frankness of conviction, Fr Ogilvie gave the judge his blessing and thanked those assembled, including the Archbishop. He shook their hands and offered them his forgiveness and, he hoped, that of God. He asked for the prayers of any hidden Catholics present, and then turned to the wall in prayer. The jury took leave for dinner. Fr Ogilvie was still on his knees when the hangman and the Sheriff returned. With incomparable humanity the martyr embraced the hangman, and said "be of good cheer" and granted him forgiveness. This gruesome trade is often forced on those who break the law, but Fr Ogilvie's executioner, like the man who was to die, was not short on the gentler feelings of humanity.

8. A Higher Power

There was an immense gathering at the scene of the execution, indicative of the impression the condemned Jesuit made on people. The expectant masses watched and waited in the High Street. Under the March sky, the gallows were erected. Up until the final minutes before his death, many tried to persuade him to renounce his faith and avoid a "death of shame". Fr Ogilvie kissed the wooden frame of the gallows. Although bound, a rosary was clutched in his hands; he took a final look at it and hurled it into the crowd. By the grace of God he found the strength to climb the steps. A Protestant minister cried to the people that "Ogilvie would die not for religion but for treason". Much offended, Fr Ogilvie shook his head and said "He does me wrong". A friend, "a devout man of humble birth" called John Abercrombie climbed up onto the platform and comforted him by saying, "No matter John, the more wrongs the better" before being thrown from the platform by the Archbishop's men. As the hangman drew near, a hush settled over the crowd. The hangman turned an apologetic face to him and said, "Do you believe in the invocation of the saints?" "Most firmly," Fr Ogilvie answered; and first in Latin and then in English, he prayed:

P. Ioannes Ogilbeus Scotus Soc: IESV, pro Catholica Religi:
one suspensus, et dissectus Glasci in Scotia, 10 Marty A. 1615.

C.S. d.   M K. f.

The Martyrdom of John Ogilvie (SJ) at Glasgow Cross, 10th March 1615.

Holy Mary, pray for us,
Holy Virgin of Virgins, pray for us
Holy Mother of God, pray for us
Saint Michael, pray for us
Saint Gabriel, pray for us
All holy Angels and Archangels, pray for us…

As the hangman put the noose over the Jesuit's head, he said, "Say John, Lord have mercy on me, Lord receive my soul". These words of supplication were acknowledged and repeated. Then the hangman thrust Fr Ogilvie from the ladder. In a final gesture of respect, he disregarded the usual custom of jumping on the hanged man's shoulders. Instead, he ran down the steps and pulled strongly on Fr Ogilvie's legs to avoid the atrocity of slow strangulation. The authorities, sensing that what had occurred had scandalised onlookers, dispensed with the usual barbarity of beheading and quartering the body. Narratives from fellow captives and those present claimed, "Those of both sexes and of all ages wept for his unjust death." The rope was cut and the martyr's lifeless body collapsed on the wooden boards. Fr Ogilvie's body was buried in an unmarked grave, possibly just outside the city, reserved for convicted criminals or those who died of the plague. His final resting place has never been identified.

Following his death, there were rumours that his body was exhumed under cover of night by a group of forty mounted horsemen. When the authorities got wind of this, they re-opened the grave and struck his (empty) coffin with a mattock. There the issue was left to rest; there was enough unease about the Jesuit. Who would want to take his body? Some suggest it was Catholic noblemen, desiring to honour him with a Christian burial. But we may never know where his remains lie, only that his soul is united with God.

After Fr Ogilvie's execution, his Catholic associates narrowly escaped death. Evidence given at the preliminary inquiries for the process of beatification in Rome (1629), where William Sinclair lived in exile, states that on 15th August 1615 William Sinclair, Robert Wilkie and Robert Cruickshanks were led to the scaffold in the High Street in Edinburgh. They were condemned for "the treasonable resettling of Jesuits and trafficking Papists". According to Sinclair:

> Three of us, by the Grace of God, were prepared to meet our death with the greatest courage. But our enemies perceived that the people were murmuring against it, and therefore the sentence of death was revoked by the King's command, and changed into one of banishment for life amid the acclamations of the bystanders.

William Sinclair (Fr Ogilvie's Edinburgh host) became a lawyer in Rome. His younger son Roger died from fever, aged fourteen. His elder son Robert followed the path of

Fr Ogilvie and studied for the priesthood with the Society of Jesus. The Heygate family were also exiled. Robert Heygate joined the army in Belgium. His younger son James, who witnessed Fr Ogilvie's death when he was twelve years old, went on to study at the Scots College in Douai and later joined the Benedictine monastery of St James at Wurzburg in Northern Bavaria. John Mayne, a fellow prisoner of the martyr, also joined the Benedictine monastery. Fr John Ogilvie, the dishonoured Jesuit, made a profound impression on many people of all ages and walks of life. There was also the case of a young nobleman from Hungary called John Eckersdorff, who was travelling through Scotland on a grand tour. Around four o'clock on 10th March, he found himself in the High Street of Glasgow, and was caught up in the tumult at the gallows. Extracts from his own account describe the scene:

> I happened to be in Scotland on the day when Fr Ogilvie was taken to the scaffold, and I can find no words to describe his proud and noble bearing as he went to death. Just before he went up the ladder he flung the rosary from the scaffold as a last souvenir for the Catholics who were near him. This rosary, flung at random, hit me in the chest, so that I had but to put out my hand to take it. The Catholics however rushed on me so violently, that I had perforce to let it go or be knocked down. At that moment nothing was further from my

mind than religion, yet from that moment I knew not one moment's peace of mind. Those rosary beads left a wound in my soul. In vain I wandered from place to place; I could find rest in none. My conscience was troubled and this thought came back to me again and again: Why did the martyr's rosary fall on me and not someone else? For many years this question presented itself to me again and again, and was with me wherever I was. Conscience won at last. I renounced Calvinism and became a Catholic. I attribute this happy conversion to the martyr's rosary (there is no other possible cause). To this rosary if I had it, I would not barter for the whole world, and for which, if anyone would offer it to me, I would give any price which they asked.

During Fr Ogilvie's captivity, this rosary was his only possession. In the course of his Jesuit training, particularly at Olmutz, he is remembered for his deep commitment to the Sodality of Our Lady, an association focused on Marian devotion. Throwing his rosary into the crowd could be perceived as a symbolic sharing of a devotional object. As Fr Ogilvie was considered a martyr, this act holds tremendous significance. The rosary would be a relic - a personal memorial of someone noted for their sanctity and holiness, hence worthy of veneration. Who claimed the rosary and what happened to it since is another unanswered question.

Fr Ogilvie's own testimony of his imprisonment and trial, *Relatio Incarcerationis*, and supplementary accounts from fellow prisoners and eye-witnesses were brought to France by John Mayne. They were printed at Douai in 1615 and other places thereafter. News of Fr Ogilvie's martyrdom spread quickly in Britain and across Europe. William Sinclair, James Heygate and John Mayne gave evidence at the first opening of the cause of Fr Ogilvie. Fr Virgilio Cepari, Procurator General of the Society of Jesus, initiated preparations for the first process of canonisation in Wurzburg, Germany (1628) and Rome (1629). However, wider issues including the suppression of the Society of Jesus (1773-1814) and the persecution of Catholics in Britain (until the gradual repeal of anti-Catholic penal laws from 1778) complicated the already lengthy and complex process of canonisation. It was almost three centuries later that the Apostolic Process opened in Glasgow on 12th July 1929, leading to beatification on 22nd December, 1929. Fr John Ogilvie was now called Blessed.

Devotion to John Ogilvie was certainly not restricted to Glasgow, but it is fair to say there was a very committed lay movement in the city. Hundreds of ordinary Catholics would celebrate the "Ogilvie Walk" from the Tolbooth up to the High Street on the anniversary of his martyrdom. The laity were also instrumental in giving evidence in the cause for beatification. There was talk of answers to prayers and claims of cures. In one particular case, Blessed

John Ogilvie was identified as the answer to prayers for a Canadian woman who recovered from breast and bone cancer. However, the findings of a subsequent investigation were inconclusive. The cause of canonisation was resumed on 8th July 1965. The process leading to full canonisation is inherently difficult, as there must be proof beyond all doubt that a miracle has taken place since the beatification.

9. "Mary, I'm Hungry"

John Fagan was a forty-nine-year-old docker who lived in Easterhouse, Glasgow. His wife, Mary, recalled how her husband would often return home from work exhausted and suffering from stomach pain, with his sandwiches uneaten. Before long, he was vomiting blood, which led to medical tests, a blood transfusion and X-rays in hospital. Mr Fagan suspected he had a stomach ulcer. On 14th May 1965, the Fagans were advised surgery was required as the X-ray had shown a massive carcinoma. The operation was complex as the cancer in the stomach had invaded the transverse colon. John Fagan's wife was cautioned that his recovery would be temporary. His doctor advised Mary, "John must never know." After a period of recuperation Mr Fagan was keen to get back to work, and by the end of the summer he had lighter duties as a checker at the docks. However by November his condition had greatly deteriorated. His local general practitioner, Dr Archibald MacDonald, suspected a mass in his patient's upper abdomen. The hospital confirmed secondary malignant tumours. Mrs Fagan was advised nothing could be done for her husband - "take him home and be good to him".

Mr Fagan spent most of his time in bed and his wife

seldom left the house. A hospice for the dying was advised, but Mary Fagan insisted, "whatever has to be done for John, I'll do it myself." She had met her husband in 1935 when she was just sixteen; they would walk together in Kelvingrove Park, go to the dancing and the pictures together. They married two years later in their local church, St Patrick's. They had six children. Joe, the eldest, returned home from Australia and Mr Fagan's brother Jim travelled from Sligo to be with the family. The tumour in the upper abdomen was steadily increasing and Mr Fagan's weight dropped to around five stone. Mrs Fagan was comforted by her children and thoughtful neighbours who helped with washing and shopping. The assistant priest from Blessed John Ogilvie Church in Easterhouse, Fr Fitzgibbon, would bring Mr Fagan Holy Communion, but by the end of January 1967 he had received the Last Rites. Fr Fitzgibbon also gave Mrs Fagan a medal of Blessed John Ogilvie which was pinned to her husband's pyjamas. He promised to ask Blessed John Ogilvie to intercede for her husband and prayers were also said during Mass. He added, "You must ask him too. It's going to take a miracle to save him, so ask Blessed John Ogilvie for that miracle."

The Legion of Mary, a group of lay parishioners who visited sick people in hospital and at home, came to pray for Mr Fagan on Sunday 5th March 1967. They specifically petitioned Blessed John Ogilvie to intercede for the dying man, but it was doubtful if Mr Fagan could hear them. By now he was semi-conscious with morphine to dull his pain. He had eaten nothing for seven weeks, and the stench of noxious vomit which filled the room was due to his stomach breaking up. Dr MacDonald called in to see his patient on the Saturday but left by saying, "I'm sorry Mrs Fagan; I'll come back on Monday to sign the death certificate." He was trying to prepare her for the impending loss of her husband. Most of that Sunday Mrs Fagan remained in the room with her husband; around midnight, she woke from a broken sleep. She thought she heard her husband. When she tried to gently move him onto his left side, he murmured. She said, "Did I hurt you John?" He whispered, "No, no - it was Aunt Annie, she asked me, are you coming, John?" This was a close aunt who had died ten years previously.

When Mrs Fagan got up to turn on the light, she got a shock when the light bulb shattered. But she remained in the dark, praying and sleeping restlessly. Around 6 a.m. she looked at her husband who lay still on the bed; there was a sense of calm in the room. She went over to him and put her head on his chest. There was no heartbeat or sound of breathing. John Fagan's ordeal was finally over. Completely exhausted, she put her head in her hands and wept. A moment later she thought she heard a voice say, "Mary, I'm hungry". Startled, she looked at her husband, and again she heard the words, "Mary, I'm hungry". In astonishment she answered him, "John, I thought you were dead!" When Dr MacDonald arrived, no death certificate was needed. Mrs Fagan told him, "My wee John has eaten a boiled egg". Her husband said, "Mary, I feel so different." He had no pain and no further drugs were necessary. Dr MacDonald looked at Mrs Fagan and said, "I do believe the hand of God is in this house." From 6th March onwards, Mr Fagan made a steady recovery. In early May, this man, who called himself a "wishy-washy" Catholic, dressed in his Sunday best and returned to Mass. The medal was still on his pyjamas and he prayed to Blessed John Ogilvie every day. The new year of 1968 brought work in a bakery, and medical tests over the next few years confirmed no evidence of a tumour.

10. Faith Rewarded

At first the word "miracle" was avoided, but rumours spread quickly about John Fagan's inexplicable cure. The case was cautiously investigated by the Easterhouse parish priest, Fr Reilly, following talks with Dr MacDonald who was confounded by the case. Then over the course of two and a half years, a team of three doctors considered all possible medical explanations for Mr Fagan's recovery from a "moribund" state. No medical explanation could be found. By the early 1970s, further scrutiny was carried out by Professor Livio Capocaccia, an Italian gastroenterology specialist, who called for more detailed analysis to probe every possible medical hypothesis. Other specialists were brought in and Mr Fagan had to endure additional medical examinations. Following medical tests at Edinburgh's Western General Hospital, Mr Fagan told his parish priest, "They've turned me inside out, so don't call me for another few months, Father." By the end of 1972, Professor Capocaccia concluded that a medical explanation could not be confirmed.

Meanwhile, the establishment of a Diocesan Tribunal was decreed by the Vatican. This would be conducted under the direction of Thomas Winning, the Auxiliary Bishop of Glasgow. Over many months, Mr Fagan and various medical, religious and lay witnesses were cross-examined under oath, on the basis of questions composed in Rome. The Sacred Congregation for the Causes of Saints then painstakingly examined every medical report, study, and item of documentation. Independent medical experts and a medical board also reviewed the case, which resulted in a positive outcome. Next Gaetano Stano, the *Promotor Fidei* or "Devil's Advocate", raised numerous objections, which were subsequently addressed. Then at last, the evidence was judged and approved by the Pope in February 1976 and endorsed by an assembly of cardinals. Thus, nine years after Mr Fagan's remarkable recovery, Blessed John Ogilvie was solemnly canonised by Pope Paul VI at St Peter's in Rome on Sunday 17th October 1976.

St John Ogilvie was honoured not simply for the miracle associated with a quiet, unassuming Glasgow man. He was a champion of the Church, a martyr for his faith and a defender of the right to religious liberty. Aged only thirty-six when he died, he was cut off in the prime of life. At the time of his trial in Glasgow, Fr John Ogilvie called himself "an ordinary Jesuit", but he went on to become Scotland's only Catholic Reformation martyr. The city of Rome would welcome thousands of pilgrims from Scotland (around fourteen chartered flights) along with others from Canada, America and different parts of Europe. When John and Mary Fagan walked with pride into St Peter's Basilica, a

Mr and Mrs Fagan during the canonisation of John Ogilvie (SJ) at St Peter's Basilica in Rome, 17th October 1976.

thunder of applause went up to greet this ordinary Scottish couple who experienced extraordinary events. During the formal rite of canonisation the congregation delighted in the words of Pope Paul VI:

> We declare and define that Blessed John Ogilvie is a Saint and we inscribe his name in the Calendar of the Saints and establish that he should be devoutly honoured among the Saints in the universal Church.

From his prison cell, every letter written by St John Ogilvie opened with the words *Pax Christi*, Latin for "the peace of Christ". Christ himself said, "Peace I bequeath to you, my own peace I give you, a peace the world cannot give, this is my gift to you. Do not let not your hearts be troubled or afraid" (Jn 14:27). God has given each of us free will. We therefore have the capacity to love, not hate; to forgive, not condemn. To have differences of opinion is inherently human, but to resort to favour or force - bribery, coercion, or surveillance, or absolutism regarding some views (considered right) over others - is tantamount to authoritarianism. Ultimately, to take a life is not to uphold a doctrine; it is simply to take a life. The imperfections of human law contradict the gentle laws of Christ, based on love, peace and justice. The wounds of the past take time to heal, and more often than not, during times of social, political and religious conflict, it is the guiltless that bear the brunt.

There is a striking painting by one of Scotland's leading artists, Peter Howson, which hangs in St Andrew's Cathedral in Glasgow. The painting depicts St John Ogilvie on the brink of a merciless death at the gallows. But in the midst of the shadows there is light, for this work also conveys a profound expression of serenity as the martyr clings more to heaven than to earth. As he "died with Christ, so shall he live with him", a faith uncompromised. It is easy to look back on the Reformation and other times of religious conflict and point to discord and division. But the painful reality is that even today, with the benefit of hindsight, we must continue to strive towards a more inclusive and just society which respects religious freedom and a diverse Christian vision. In October 2014, Pope Francis, the first Jesuit to lead the Catholic Church, addressed thousands of pilgrims during his weekly general audience. He called for unity among Christians and said "divisions among Christians wound Jesus as they wound the Church." Therefore we should not "Fix our look on what divides us, but rather on that which unites us, seeking to know and to love Jesus better and to share the richness of his love".

Church leaders in general would, one hopes, endorse his closing point regarding Christian fellowship:

Dear friends, let us go forward now towards full unity! History has separated us, but we are on the way towards reconciliation and communion! And when the goal might seem too distant, almost unreachable, and we feel prey to discouragement, let us be encouraged by the idea that God cannot close his ear to the voice of his son Jesus, and will hear his and our prayer, that all Christians be truly one.

May the life and death of St John Ogilvie encourage us to foster the common ground between us rather than our differences.

Prayer to St John Ogilvie

Dear St John Ogilvie
By your devotion to Christ
You held fast to faith, even unto martyrdom.
With the Grace of God,
May I have a loving heart.
In the midst of trials, may I, like you,
'Be of good cheer'
And trust in the love of God.

Please hear my prayer…

Amen.

Sources

Direct quotations in the narrative are taken from:

Relatio Incarcerationis, the martyr's own account of his trial and imprisonment: cited in W. E. Brown, *John Ogilvie: An Account of his Life and Death*. London, Burns, Oates & Washbourne, 1925.

Miracle: the cure of a Glasgow man from cancer that led to a canonisation in Rome, by Des Hickey and Gus Smith. London, Hodder and Stoughton, 1978.

Canonizzazione del Beato Giovanni Ogilvie, SJ, 17th October 1976. Printed in Italian and English. www.vatican.va

Picture Credits

Sketch of John Ogilvie by Charles Weld, courtesy of The Governors of Stonyhurst College, Lancashire.

Portrait of King James VI of Scotland and I of England, courtesy of the National Portrait Gallery, London.

Portrait of John Spottiswoode, Archbishop of Saint Andrews, courtesy of National Portrait Gallery, London.

Engraving of the martyrdom of St John Ogilvie, courtesy of the Archives of the Society of Jesus, (British Province) Mount Street, London.

Photograph of John Fagan at the canonisation of John Ogilvie St Peter's Basilica, Rome, courtesy of Eleanor McDowell.